SEVERAL MEANS OF INCOME

READ! REFLECT! EXECUTE!

DEBORAH BEYIOKU
Trouble-Shooting Expert

ABOUT THE AUTHOR

Growing up in a community that thrived and survived on micro industries gave me a hands-on approach to business from a very early stage in life. I couldn't think of a time that I was not involved with more than one business at a time.

Inspiration
Sometimes, people tell me that I do too many things; I used to think that they could be right but all that stopped after I read Spencer Johnson's **'Who moved my cheese'**; a book that I recommend for everyone to read at least once in their lifetime. If you never want to be 'caught with your pants down', financially that is, I believe that when it comes to our income, we should apply the idea of 'when one door closes another door opens'!

Education
I have been blessed with a mother that left a legacy of "get an education, no matter what you want to do for a living". Her legacy has motivated me into qualifying as a financial and legal professional, and I have merged my knowledge in both sectors to become a specialist in troubleshooting for business management, finance and law.

This book '**Several Means of Income**' draws from my experience in providing consulting services to multiple industries, from start-up organisations and businesses ranging from legal firms, pharmaceuticals, hotels to indie record labels and many more.

Hands-on the Job
As the CEO of Ochu Group limited (a global business management consultancy company), I have helped entrepreneurs to venture into new business territories as well as turning passions into lucrative businesses, through my business blog and direct consultancy.

My desire to promote and protect the welfare of others has prompted my involvement with various charities. Such as the Grow Movement, a Non-Governmental Organisation (NGO) that alleviates poverty, by helping entrepreneurs build their businesses. Through the services of volunteer mentor entrepreneurs and as a result the entrepreneurs run their businesses more effectively. This increases profits and creates jobs in their various communities. Sometimes, as the need arises, I do sponsor Non-Governmental Organisations (NGOs), as well as lending my professional services and funds to humanitarian courses globally. One of such NGOs is Mercy

Widows and Orphans Foundation, they empower widows by training them on a skill and provide them with start-up funds.

Reaching out to improve people's financial positions is as much my passion, as it is my means of income!!!

SEVERAL MEANS OF INCOME
Copyright © 2020 by Deborah Beyioku
ISBN – 978-1-838 2020-02

All Rights Reserved. This book cannot be reproduced fully or in part for any form of use without written permission of the author. For permission requests, write to the author at address: Ochu Group Consultancy Ltd, 85 Great Portland Street, First Floor, London W1W 7LT
www.ochugroupconsultancy.com
Email: info@ochugroupconsultancy.com

LIMITS OF LIABILITIES/DISCLAIMER OF WARRANTY: The author and publisher of this book have used their best efforts in preparing this material. The author and publisher disclaim any warranties (expressed or implied), or merchantability for any purpose. The author and publisher shall in no event be held liable for any loss or other damages, including, but not limited to special, incidental, consequential, or other damages. The information presented in this publication is compiled from sources believed to be accurate at the time of printing, however, the publisher assumes no responsibility for errors and omissions. The information in this publication is not intended to replace or substitute professional advice. The author and publisher specifically dismissed any liability, loss, or risk that is incurred consequently, directly of the use and application of any of the content of this information.

Ochu Group Ltd bears no responsibility for the accuracy of the information on any website cited and/or used by the author in this book. The inclusion of website address in this book does not constitute an endorsement by, or associate Ochu group ltd with such sites or the content, products, advertising, or other materials presented.

Opinions expressed by the author do not necessarily represent the views and opinion of Ochu Group Ltd. The publisher assumes no liability for any content or opinion expressed by, or through the author.

CONTENTS

TESTIMONIALS xii
ACKNOWLEDGEMENT xvi
FOREWORD xviii
INTRODUCTION 1

Chapter 1: **PRE-STARTING STAGE** 4
- Week 1
- Week 2
- Week 3

Chapter 2: **SOURCING FUNDS FOR YOUR BUSINESS** 11
- Uncommon lending methods
- Identify the service area that that needs improvement Ideal funding for export business
- Decide what is best for your business

Chapter 3: **BEING THE BOSS OF YOU** 20
- Self-Appraisal
- Identify your goals and focus
- Source competitors in your domain
- Check if professional training is required.

Chapter 4: **LIVE OFF YOUR PASSION** 30
- Identifying your unique strength
- Identifying your inspirations
- Identify your experience
- Quantifying your value
- Join forces with like minds

- Get in-action

Chapter 5: **LIVING ON A BUDGET** 37
- Selling clutter
- Home School the Children
- Grown your food
- Keep off name brand products
- Stick to necessary spending
- Start a small business

Chapter 6: **FREELANCE COURT ARTIST** 45
- Apply a professional attitude
- Develop a unique style of work
- Research other court Artists
- Locate the court you want to work in
- Source your customers
- Maintain media presence

Chapter 7: **PERFUME MAKING BUSINESS**......52
- Research
- Get Perfume making supplies
- Brand your products
- Survey your market
- Register your business
- Impact on others

Chapter 8: **RUNNING AN INDIE RECORD LABEL** 59
- Sourcing your team of music-artist
- Finding a lawyer
- Registering the business
- Sourcing funding
- Setting up a studio

- Joining music business association

Chapter 9: ART GALLERY BOSS 66
- Business planning
- Searching for artists
- Finding business premises
- Registering the gallery
- Applying marketing strategy
- Launching the gallery

Chapter 10: BUSINESS TO BUSINESS TEAMWORK 75
- Associations
- Joint venture
- Planned alliances
- Affiliates marketing
- Conjunction
- Deal making

Chapter 11: KEEPING YOUR BUSINESS FINANCIALLY AFOOT 80
- Freeing your store off old stock
- Offering a discount to your debtors
- Offering gift vouchers to customers
- Offering subscriptions
- Offering special deals to customers
- Venturing into new markets

Chapter 12: SUSTAINING YOUR BUSINESS 85
- Business premises
- Health and safety (H&S)

- Fire protection & waste management
- Getting stock
- Staff structure

Chapter 13: **YOUR BUSINESS GOLD**............93
- Conducting frequent surveys
- Do not sound desperate
- Strategize negotiating process
- Enhance service/products at intervals
- Prioritise all sections of the business
- Know your product/services

Chapter 14: **YOU CAN BE RICH AND HAPPY**........................100
- Avoid negative ideas
- Consider how your business can benefit others
- Identify the market gap in your community
- Identify employment gap in your community
- Love your business
- Make time for your family

MY FINAL THOUGHTS............................107

TESTIMONIALS

It has always been great to associate with Debbie who works tirelessly with an aim of improving the lives of others. She is passionate and ready to part her skills to the would-be entrepreneurs. I am inspired by her work and looking forward to how others will benefit from this!!

William
(*Malawi*)

The taste is in the pudding. Deborah is very professional in setting realistic goals to support and ensure my business goals or needs are accomplished on time. I recommend her and encourage you to read her books and seek her support.

Abo
(*Graphic Designer, London*)

Debbie is inspiration and motivation personified, impacting her generation positively. Revealed within the book are secrets for business breakthroughs and successful living. I recommend it to everyone.

Livy-Elcon Emereonye
(*Pharmacist, Public Health Analyst, Publisher and Author of Path of Fulfilment and more*)

Debbie is a passion driven woman who is a lovely inspiration in business. She wants to give the best of herself in everything she does, and this book is not an exception.

Vicky Ovedje
(Health care professional, London)

I find this book to be very inspirational. I would even present it as a gift to people in my community. Food for thought!

Magdalene
(*CEO Nyayia maternity hospital,* Sierra Leone)

A simply structured and informative book with a realistic business ideology, suitable for those wishing to start-up their own business or expand an existing one. It contains inspiring, motivating and encouraging ideas. A good book for a person with a business creative mind. The Author is an enthusiastic and courageous lady, with high ambition to inspire and encourage others to achieve their business goal within a globe market. I would recommend her book to any business entrepreneur, wishing to acquire knowledge on setting-up business and raising finance. Therefore, the information within the book should be adhered with.

Jessica Timothy
(Proprietor of Tots & Pre-school, London)

The author, Deborah Beyioku passionately details the basics plus much more in the easiest to read and engaging format of methodical steps and processes. The idea of the notes section at the end of each chapter; prompts us to reflect and put into practice what we've read and learnt...This evidences the author is not letting us off easy, she wants us to execute and succeed! As part owner of a local community family business, I can very much relate to the writer's experience and advice, particularly having had to learn these business attributes in a painstakingly long-winded way. I wish Deborah Beyioku had written this book much earlier! However, in reading this 'Several Means of Income', I have picked up some excellent tips for the future growth of our own business. If only to prove we can be rich and happy too...Chapter 14.

Yvonne Watkins-Knight
(Business Partner, Clean & Handy Services, London)

DEDICATION

This piece of work is dedicated to the greatest author of all time, The ALMIGHTY GOD 'JEHOVAH'

ACKNOWLEDGEMENT

My sincere appreciation is to my lovely parents Nwaeleweura and Ochu for embedding culture, determination and confidence in me as a child. That sense of belonging has strengthened me to believe that anything is possible.

I am ever so grateful to God for my 3 nations, my children Chika, Kelechi and Chioma, that HE gave to the world through me. However, for this piece of work, I must say, a special thanks to you, my beautiful 'Ada (first daughter)' for challenging me into writing this book within a short space of time.

I live my life each day wanting to learn from everyone and everything that I come across, even obstacles, personally, I consider them as an acquired knowledge. Whether watching a film or reading a book, I am all about retaining knowledge and drawing inspiration from both encouraging words and even those not deemed encouraging by the prudent man.

Therefore, I am thankful for everyone that I have come across in my journey of life, for it was my God's wish for you to cross my path, the authors that have inspired me over the years, motivators and speakers that have led training programs to share their ideas and experiences with others, including me.

Finally, my sincere appreciation to everyone that has purchased this book. Whether you are a young mother or a pensioner, employed or unemployed, an undergraduate or a graduate, I hope that this book motivates you into running your business better if you're already in business or creating several means of income.

ENJOY READING, REFLECTING AND EXECUTING!!!

FOREWORD

After many years in the financial industry running branches for a well-known, high street bank, I retired in 2014. The first thing I did in retirement was to realise one of my dreams and signed up to college to learn 'balloon artistry'. I gained my qualification. Being very creative and with a love for organisation led me to starting up a small 'Events' business with my sisters.

One of my favourite quotes is from President Obama's election victory speech in 2008 and the popular campaign chant 'Yes we can!'

Dreams really can come true, it doesn't matter how old or young you are, if you truly believe, and put in the necessary work 'you really can'.

I first met Deborah in 2009 when I started going to St. Anne's Church in Southwark. Deborah and I became connected through fellowship and over the years our relationship grew stronger and she has inspired me in many ways. Ever since getting to know her she is always helping someone to accomplish their vision whether here in the UK or in her country of birth, giving her support in any way she can to make dreams come true. Deborah also runs a monthly business networking seminar helping businesses get connected. Yes, Deborah has a 'can do attitude' and a passion for what she does.

So, your dream is to start your own business, you have your product/service, you have done your market research, looked at the local demographics and identified your target market and have your business plan, so what next?

In this new age of small, medium business entrepreneurship, 'Several Means of Income' provides valuable information and guidelines that covers the necessary stages of a start-up business, simplifying a complicated subject. The Author holds your hand and guides you through, the early financial planning stage, the sourcing of funds, the pitfalls and loopholes of lending whether from a high street bank or the local Credit Union, as well as the legalities of starting your own business - this book covers it all.

Deborah has a passion for business and has all the qualities needed to support anyone who has ever dreamt of starting their own business.

What's holding you back? You've already taken your first step to achieving your dream, read this book and climb the ladder to success ...**believe**.... Yes, we can!

Dreams really can come true!

Jennifer P Weise-Henry
August 2020

SEVERAL MEANS OF INCOME

Introduction

Sometimes the only thing holding us back is the idea of waiting to start big and to do that you need massive funding which is not always the case should you want to start small. But nothing stops you from starting right now! Right here! After all, some of the successful businesses we know started small, for example, Sainsbury's was established in 1869, by John James Sainsbury and his wife Mary Ann, selling fresh foods from a street shop. On a similar note, in 1976 Anita Roddick started The Body Shop as a small outfit in Brighton, selling just 25 products, both companies and many more like them, that started small, have grown into multi-million companies.

This book provides you with some practical and realistic ideas to help you start small and seize the opportunity to get to the top. No more excuses. "Dig in and turn your passion or experiences into a career." Gain your freedom, your financial and emotional independence is for you to take.

No one will hand it to you but you! In this book, there is something for everyone at all stages and levels of life; ideas that an ongoing business can apply to progress the business. There are also

DEBORAH BEYIOKU

ideas to encourage start-ups to take the first step, remember:

"A Journey of a Thousand Miles begins with a Single step" Lao Tzu

Whether you are in gainful employment, employed unemployed, between-jobs, a pensioner, or a student, reading this book will get you thinking of plan B, if you haven't yet figured out one.

In this book you will also be directed to organisations that your business may require to get help and get you started.

Chapters 1 to 2 takes you through the actions you need to take before starting your business.

Chapter 3 takes you through the benefits of owning and running your own business.

Chapter 4 gets you to reflect on yourself, as in how valuable your abilities and capabilities are, natural gift or what you are 'blessed with' if you are 'a person of faith' like me.

Chapter 5 is about self and family management.

SEVERAL MEANS OF INCOME

Chapters 6 to 9 suggest and direct your attention to businesses that you could start with next to nothing capital.

Chapters 10 to 14 direct you on how you can better keep your business progressing steadily and sustainably.

At the end of each chapter, there will be pages for you to take down notes of your proposed actions, prompted from that chapter.

Finally, you will have the opportunity to start your budget notes that will help provide you with a realistic understanding of your present financial position; especially useful to those yet to start a business.

On reading **'Several Means of Income'** you will realise that it's not just a text to be read and dropped, but a guide and directory to be followed or referred to at different stages of running your business.

DEBORAH BEYIOKU

Chapter 1

Pre-Starting stage

At a stage in our lives, we tend to be employed, it's the starting stage of most adults but this shouldn't be anyone's long term plan, especially in these days of financial uncertainty. We can no longer rely on a pension scheme that might not be available when we need it in the most vulnerable stage of our lives and if available, might not even be sustainable.

SEVERAL MEANS OF INCOME

Now is the time to start and we mustn't wait till we can start big, rather we should start small and grow, that's the fact of life. The thriving businesses that we see today started small, as I mentioned earlier in the introduction.

Start with what I call a business meeting with 'ME, MYSELF AND I'

This should take about 30mins of your time weekly, at least, and make sure to note down your ideas. Asking yourself questions and providing the best possible and sincere answers. You start in the following order:

Week 1

- List the reasons why you want to start a business.

- How would starting a business add to your growth as a person, possibly to that of your family and community?

- What are you good at doing without adding much stress to yourself and not imprisoning yourself in pursuit of running your own business?

DEBORAH BEYIOKU

- Who are your potential customers and is there a need for your service or product in your proposed marketplace?

- How would you value and respect the time invested into the business as you would for the capital invested in the business?

- How would you designate the time for business and stick to it?

Week 2

- Start with a mental survey of an existing problem that a customer in your proposed industry is having and how your service could be a possible solution to the problem.

- After working out the above at this meeting with 'ME, MYSELF AND I,' then you could start reaching out to some actual potential customers, to get their opinion on the service or product that you plan to provide.

- Now think of your capital, if you are in employment, do you have enough money saved for the proposed business?

- Do you have to borrow from family, friends, government grant schemes or financial institutions, for example banks?

SEVERAL MEANS OF INCOME

- Whatever you decide, if getting a grant proves impossible, it is always better to start with personal savings or family loans, as this will help avoid having to pay huge interest, which can be stressful for a beginner.

Week 3

- Consider the location of your business operation, whether from your home or renting a premise outside your home.

- Consider whether you have enough funding and for how long, to pay for the premises, if working from outside your home?

- And the needed equipment to enable operations.

Now make a list of your foreseeable expenses, to avoid any unpleasant surprises when your business is up and running. Ensure to conduct a research into what is required to start your business and make a list of your foreseeable expenses, starting with:

- If you plan to operate your business from home, list the possible changes or additions to accommodate your business needs within your home.

- If you plan to rent, you must ensure that you have enough funding to sustain this rent for at least three to six months, make necessary adjustments on the suit your business purpose.

- If you have opted for a lease (most likely, longer term of renting) be sure to have enough funding for the necessary improvements on the location, by pre-costing the material and labour before signing any contracts.

- Should your business require that you purchase a property, you must seriously consider cost in relation to purchase survey and plan construction or remodelling costs; which are mainly materials, labour, land tax etc. depending on the property or business law of the country where your business will be located. This is a major business decision and should not be made blindly.

When you have sorted the kind of goods or service that you want to provide, the location from which to reach your customers or clients. Then the next stage should be to make a list of some necessities:

1. Cost for interior equipment, such as computers, printers, types of machinery etc.

SEVERAL MEANS OF INCOME

depending on your kind of operations but these are just the basics.

2. Cost management expenses, such as renewal and servicing of rent, lease or mortgage, utility bills, business rate, consultancy fees, insurance payment, staff salaries.

All of which should be tailored to your business and available funds.

Every business, especially new businesses, needs a public domain presence or else it is like a book left on the shelf to gather dust and never read. To avoid such waste of time and resources, a business needs to set aside advertisement and promotional budgets.

Expenses for signposting, material for printing newsletters, brochures and even travel cost are all recurring costs. When first venturing into a new business, it might be difficult and tricky to get a proposed budget right. It is prudent to make budgetary allowance for incidentals and eventualities due to unforeseeable changes in the market.

DEBORAH BEYIOKU

TAKE NOTES OF PROPOSED ACTIONS PROMPTED BY THIS CHAPTER

Reader's Reflection:

_____
_____
_____
_____
_____
_____

Execution Method

_____
_____
_____
_____
_____
_____

Deadline for completion (Execute)

_____
_____
_____
_____
_____
_____

SEVERAL MEANS OF INCOME

Chapter 2

Sourcing funds for your business

The joy of finally realising what you want to do for a business is a good feeling but that feeling can easily be paused by the reality of not having access to adequate capital to fund the business. If you are considering a solution to that lack of capital, then you must meet the common lenders' expectation of you as a business owner. This means having a credible business profile, a business plan containing a realistically presented forecast, your initial cash investment, and your willing pledge (as in security) to the proposed lenders for the loan. When you have all these in place, then you are more likely to secure a loan for your business.

DEBORAH BEYIOKU

You start sourcing capital for your business by researching your potential lenders and weighing each of their lending requirements, terms and condition against your kind of business to know which best meets your needs. You should:

- Consider your business plan and financial forecast against your possible loan repayment amount.

- Note what you have already invested in terms of equipment, premises and possibly money in the bank, if any.

- Separate that from what you already have, then you will realise the actual amount that you need to borrow.

Most lenders will want to know your business capabilities and financial worth before offering you a loan, a mortgage, a grant or an overdraft for short-term and credit card for covering temporary cash flow problems. That is why you need a strategic and detailed business plan to reduce the risk of borrowing money that you are not sure of what to actually do with it and as a result, may not be making enough money to cover the loan repayment, plus the interest on the loan.

Below are some of the alternative roots you can explore when sourcing funding for your business.

SEVERAL MEANS OF INCOME

Uncommon Lending Methods

Most people are familiar with the usual high street banks and their lending methods and requirements. There are equally alternative lending methods that are not commonly known but are accessible to businesses, if you meet their requirements, example of these are:

- Financial Houses that provide businesses with hire purchases and rental agreements for vehicles, equipment, stock, raw materials and possibly credit insurance.

- Venture Capital firms that help start-up businesses and provides support for established businesses. You can access such firms by visiting
https://angelinvestmentnetwork.co.uk/investors

- Prince's Trust provides funding and training to young entrepreneurs in the UK. They also assist young entrepreneurs with marketing, counselling and advice. For more information, visit their website
https://www.princes-trust.org.uk

- Credit Unions or Cooperatives can provide small business loans to help businesses within communities. You can access one of these credit unions on www.militarycu.uk, this organisation provides loans that are tailored to meet their members' needs. You can access cooperatives on www.co-operativebank.co.uk

- Business angels are willing investors searching for young businesses to invest in. Terms and conditions of lending and repayment is based on special arrangements between the parties. Their web sites will provide more information www.angelinvestmentnetwork.co.uk and www.nibusinessinfo.co.uk. Find your local network meeting at UK Business Angels Association www.ukbaa.org.uk

- The Community Development Finance Associations that provide new businesses in disadvantaged communities with funds for expansion. Check them out at www.cdfa.org.uk.

If all these do not suit your business, there is always the oldest lending association "Friends and Family." Although approachable and can be informal, I recommend that you be as formal as possible by declaring any possible risk. In order to eliminate any delay or complications with repayment.

Small business grants and Loans arrangements

To encourage economic growth, most governments make funds available for start-up and small businesses through grant and loan schemes, often, the business owners are not aware of this support

SEVERAL MEANS OF INCOME

or how to access it. Such grants or loans are made through:

- Governments' Departments of Trade and Industry, European Union, regional development agencies, local councils and possibly, community enterprise groups, grant-making trust. To make inquiries about ongoing grants or loans and how to apply, log in to www.grantsonline.org.uk for updates on these opportunities.

- The UK government periodically makes almost £3,000.00 in grants and over £50,000 in loans accessible to businesses. There could be similar provisions in other countries or government.

- To keep up to date on requirements and procedure for grants and loans, register free online at www.j4grants.co.uk and through their newsletters, they will inform you about new grants and closing date.

Most businesses that settle for small loan arrangements, often never qualify for a grant and interest on loans is low compared to high street banks. However, a loan is not to be rushed into, regardless. If possible, keep to lenders with a government guarantee against defaults.

Identify the service area that needs improvement

It is imperative to identify the area of business that you need invest the loan and the best possible kind of loan to acquire. It will be a waste of money to be paying back a loan that is not beneficial to the business. In order to identify the key area for improvement, consider:

- Access to needed equipment (especially vehicles) without having to worry about purchasing it with capital that the business cannot afford.

- Equipment financiers, being responsible for the cost of maintenance.

- Rentals being regarded as Tax-deductible items.

- Hired equipment costing less as financiers can claim back VAT on purchase.

Ideal funding for export business

In the United Kingdom, some banks provide a special a special payment security for small exporters, this might be available in other countries and it does not hinder them from accessing other loans or keeping to prior loan agreements. It's done through the following process:

SEVERAL MEANS OF INCOME

- Banks release the funds when an export order is shipped and hold the right documents lodged.

- Released funds could be up to 100% of invoice value excluding interest and transaction fee or associated cost.

- If you, as the customer default on their payment, the bank would not come after you as the funding comes as a package with an insurance cover.

- The insurance helps to lower the interest charges for the business.

A similar provision comes in the form of promissory notes (containing recipient's name, agreed sum and dates), commonly known as IOUs (I Owe You) which is usually an informal document acknowledging debt. However, it's worth making inquiries with the bank.

Also, when purchasing any item from abroad, a credit letter from your bank could serve as an internationally agreed method of payment that will enable you to get-off with not paying for the goods before shipping.

Decide what is best for your business

Now you have full knowledge of different kinds of grants and loans providers, including "Bank of

Family and Friends". Find out what each of them requires from you before they can grant or loan you the funds to run your business. Always state clearly what the fund will be used for. Therefore, you need to present the lenders with these:

- A detailed explanation of what you intend to do with the fund, whether for a start-up or existing business expansion.

- Explain your implementation strategy.

- State the cost of this new idea, how much you already have, if any and how much you are asking them to lend you.

- And how you plan to pay it back, should it be a loan and not a grant.

You must consider your business interest over that of the lender when borrowing, but that is not to say that you should expect the lenders to allow you to have an undue advantage over them. As always, never fail to include how your new business ideas will economically impact on your community. That is the right thing to do and it will also impress both your grant and loan providers.

SEVERAL MEANS OF INCOME

TAKE NOTES OF PROPOSED ACTIONS PROMPTED BY THIS CHAPTER

Reader's Reflection:

_____
_____
_____
_____
_____
_____

Execution Method

_____
_____
_____
_____
_____
_____

Deadline for completion (Execute)

_____
_____
_____
_____
_____
_____

Chapter 3

Being the boss of you

The minute you think about being the 'Boss of you' is when you begin to get a sense of freedom, (Getting to the next stage is the beginning of the end of the stagnant daily life,) But not without the challenges that come with owning your own business, as you will find with any adventure. Identifying an industry to focus on and strategizing your method and sticking to it may be difficult. Though it might be an industry that you have gained experience in, as an employee, you still need to start by considering your capabilities and resilience.

SEVERAL MEANS OF INCOME

Optimism is an essential factor when starting a business, but one should also be realistic and pessimistic to an extent. These 3 factors help any boss prepare and plan, especially when things do not go as planned within an expected time. However, it's ideal to consider these set-ups:

Self-Appraisal
Conducting an aptitude appraisal should be the starting point to enabling one to identify certain useful skills and habits that might help you in becoming a successful boss. *The skill to:*

- Function under pressure whilst being calm, cool and collected

- Make quick and important decisions with set positive outcomes

- Influence and lead people.

- Strive to be independent with financial freedom, as a means to an end.

- Being adventurous yet not deliberately avoiding changes and challenges.

- Be zealous to accomplish a task, no matter how difficult.

- Communicate ideas in an easily understandable manner whilst considering another person's opinion.

- Separate business from family responsibilities and accord the necessary time to either side.

Tip**

Anyone venturing out into owning a business must be a people person, the expected aim of any business is to be successful, create employment, and possibly reduce unemployment. It is commonly known that an employed community produces happy people and buoyant economy.

Identify Your Goal and Focus
The hunger to change a situation could be the main drive to progressing and reaching a goal in a self-owned business. You need to make the best use of the expected benefit; focus on the positive change you want to achieve by being your own boss.

5 Golden opportunities that will help your drive

- The opportunity to manage your own time and do things that you have always wanted to do.

- The opportunity to financially afford your expensive hobbies and leisure.

SEVERAL MEANS OF INCOME

- The opportunity to be debt-free, within a short period of being your own boss.

- The opportunity to employ others, thereby growing the economy within your community.

- The opportunity to nurture and grow something (business) that could even benefit future generations.

You should be aware that, in the real sense, there is no 'BOSS' in business, and the real `BOSS' is the end service users. These are customers/clients, depending on the nature of your business, they bring in the money and if they are not happy with your product delivery, the business cannot progress. So, to sustain business progression, we focus on identifying potential risks, and then devise a method to avoid it. Frequent SWOT (Strength, Weakness, Opportunities and Threats) analysis of who you are as a 'Boss', is equally as important as that of your business. It should go together; as for an analysis of your employees, this is obtained through appraisals.

DEBORAH BEYIOKU

Source Competitors in your Domain

Unless you intend on going down the route of being an inventor, bear in mind that any business you are getting into already has someone in similar business. It is important to look into what people in similar business around you are offering their customers; then think of how you can provide same in product or service but in an improved and unique way; whilst enjoying what you do. If you don't, running the business would stress you and no money is worth a threat to one's health and wellbeing. To achieve the balance of health and business success, I suggest you take the 4 golden ideas into consideration.

4 Golden ideas...

- The idea of considering what your leisure is and merging it into your new business.

- The idea of considering past jobs or positions and merging it into your new business.

- The idea of considering businesses that are in demand, then provide the product/service, uniquely.

SEVERAL MEANS OF INCOME

- The idea of considering the purchasing of an already established business or buying into the franchise.

If you choose to engage your leisure and ideas from your previous jobs; it is paramount for your ideas to focus on providing your customers with their demands whilst making profits from the business. The obvious means of doing that is providing value for money in the form of product and services.

Check if professional training is required

As soon as you decide of the area of business that you want to focus on, you must verify licensing requirement of the trade. You may need to continuously update yourself with further training if you were previously trained in that industry. Then find out whether it is a type of trade that requires you to belong to a professional body or subject to regulations and licenses. For instance, businesses like owning a:

- Pharmacy requires professional training and licensing

- Restaurant requires that you register the local council office of where the business will be located, obtain food hygiene & safety certificate as well as alcohol license if you intend to serve alcohol on the premises

- Financial advisory service requires certification and is regulated by the Financial Conduct Authority
- Transport or delivery business requires proper driver and vehicle insurance
- Private security firm is regulated by the Security Industry Authority (SIA) and a valid certificate and badge a requirement in the United Kingdom
- A law firm principal needs to be an admitted member of the (SRA) Solicitors Regulations Authority, and the firm registered with the SRA.
- Business that involves caring/education of children need to register with the Office for the Standard Education Department (**Ofsted**).

Businesses that need to keep peoples' information/data, whether as customers or staffs, must fulfil the requirements of the Data Protection Act 2018, by registering with the Information Commissioner's Office (ICO).

Solidify your Goal

When you are certain about the nature of the trade that you wish to go into, the next step would be to

SEVERAL MEANS OF INCOME

make a list of the services of the business you can provide. Such services could be driven by skill you had acquired through training or past work experiences. This could be skills acquired through:

- Day to day administrative/managerial knowledge gained through training or experience.

- Basic book-keeping knowledge gained through training or experience.
- Marketing/customer service knowledge gained through training or experience.

- Negotiating knowledge gained through training or experience.

- Logistic knowledge gained through training or experience.

- Research/Survey knowledge gained through training or experience.

Advance awareness of the skills and services helps you know and plan for the possible limitations you may have in providing certain professional services and the cost to the business. Do not hesitate to hire certain professional help as and when the need arises.

DEBORAH BEYIOKU

Most crucial is the professional input of an Accountant and a branding/marketing expert, as the business progresses. Regulatory awareness is also important, to help with constant adjustment of the business capabilities when necessary.

Impact on your chosen Industry

Now, it is time to break out, stand-up and be counted in your chosen line of business you need to start making your mark and your impact. By reaching out to groups that are beneficial to the business, for instance:

- Social media, by posting business activities.

- Joining similar business societies or associations for constant updates in the industry.

- Keep-up with local authority entrepreneur forums.

It is all about improving yourself as an employer and for your employees, through training and educational programmes.

SEVERAL MEANS OF INCOME

TAKE NOTES OF PROPOSED ACTIONS PROMPTED BY THIS CHAPTER

Reader's Reflection:

_____
_____
_____
_____
_____
_____

Execution Method

_____
_____
_____
_____
_____
_____

Deadline for completion (Execute)

_____
_____
_____
_____
_____
_____
_____

Chapter 4

Live off your passion

One of the keyways of making a living off your passion is to start by asking yourself the key questions, who am I, a sheep, or a shepherd? If you think you are a sheep, then halt and seek professional help on building your confidence; but if you consider yourself a shepherd, then take shepherd-like actions.

SEVERAL MEANS OF INCOME

The idea is to take the needed action to develop your passion which will, in turn, provide you with sustainable means of income. Some actions that might help you develop your passion includes...

Identifying your unique strength

- Think about your strengths and how it could help your business. Focus on one key strength or talent from the start. A multi-talented altitude could hamper your uniqueness, it is much better to start one business after another.

- It's that ideal uniqueness that gives you an edge over your competitors in business; leaving you fulfilled, knowing that you are starting on a good note which is adding value and positive results to your business.

- The saying "nothing is new under the sun" doesn't just apply to inventions because business delivery strategy could be unique within an industry when identified and applied.

Identifying your inspirations

- Identifying that thing that put a smile on your face when you think of it because you can't wait to get out of bed each day to do that thing.

- You need to dig out what inspires you from among your multi passions by being true to yourself.

- Inspirations are often an activity of a sort, that one, that takes you to your happiest moment when in action.

- When you have identified it, apply a strategy to turn it into a business.

- Business goals and objectives are easier met when the initial ideas for the business are inspired by passion.

Identify your experience

- Experience may help you have an edge over your competitors in business, as in providing better products and services to your customers.

- Reflect on your past experiences, make a list and cross them out starting from the one you least enjoyed. Select and apply experience that is adequate for your business, that is the key to success.

- Although there are no rules prohibiting people without experience from running businesses, having experience could help avoid minor or major mistakes in your business.

SEVERAL MEANS OF INCOME

- Experience gained not only through work but through life, could be handy in running your business.

Quantify your value

- Quantifying your value requires total consideration of your **(TPPSC)** Time, Professional-worth, Production and Service Cost). Compare the services or products that you are to provide, against that of your proposed competitors, the cost of your service against the cost of your competitors' service.

- No one knows your value more than you do and if you do not place a value on yourself and possibly your products and services no one would, after all, why should anyone pay for your services when you can provide it for free.

- Every line of business or trade has its method of quantifying this value, although it may prove difficult, it's important for any business that wishes to make a profit.

Join forces with like minds

- Sometimes joining forces could just be between two individuals with a similar passion to turn it into business. Finding like-minded people (opens an avenue for joint venture) could fill a missing gap on both spectra that could enable the achievement of mutual goals.

- This will reduce the struggles that a starter business is likely to face as it provides access to new markets, experience contacts and possibly funding, depending on the needs of both parties.

- Another form of joining forces could be in association with a different kind of business that could compensate others' businesses, possibly by both businesses using incentives to direct customers to each other.

- Call it a joint venture, association, affiliates, depending on the parties, but it does not have to be indefinite; it could be for a while.

- It is advisable to state the terms in a joint venture agreement before coming together.

Get in-action

- You have identified your passion, organised how to make it a means of living.

- You have chosen a part of the establishment, whether sole trader or incorporated, you will be required to file yearly tax.

SEVERAL MEANS OF INCOME

- You have done your research and identified the gap in the market to be filled.
- Now get in-action and inject the market with your services.

I hope this motivates you to live off your passion and do log in to www.ochugroupconsultancy.com for further assistance with starting or growing your business.

DEBORAH BEYIOKU

TAKE NOTES OF PROPOSED ACTIONS PROMPTED BY THIS CHAPTER

Reader's Reflection:
_____
_____
_____
_____
_____
_____

Execution Method
_____
_____
_____
_____
_____

Deadline for completion (Execute)
_____
_____
_____
_____
_____
_____

SEVERAL MEANS OF INCOME

Chapter 5

Living on a budget

Running your home on a budget is not restricted to people with less money, as any home without a budget is deemed reckless, mismanaged, and unstructured and often likely to fail. The same applies to a company without a business plan, an office manual and other logistic tools needed for a functioning business.

DEBORAH BEYIOKU

Logging onto www.realsimple.com/work-life/family/business will help give families a head-start on managing their affairs. Family units need to come up with contingency plan in organising and directing their finances by:

Selling clutter

Clutter is unused items (clothing, shoes, bags, appliances and more) that gather dust in your home, and you have not used in a while nor have any plans to use them anytime soon. Luckily for someone on a budget, there are several ways of turning those items into cash.

- Car boot sale - Selling your old stuff from your car boot, at a designated Saturday or Sunday market, it's quite common in the United Kingdom.

- Garage sale - Selling your old or unwanted items from your home garage, which is a common practice in the United States of America.

- Sell through the internet, on platforms like E-bay or Facebook, for those with access and knowledge of the internet, this would require a camera to take photos of items, internet access and a local post office to deliver the sold packages to your buyers.

SEVERAL MEANS OF INCOME

Home School the Children

Home-schooling your children may not be necessary in a country that provides free, quality and compulsory education to minors. But where such provisions are not freely accessible, then it's important to provide quality education from your home if possible or you will need to:

- Set up the right study programme for the child's age and include day trips (excursions), as education is not only in books but also in your surroundings.

- Invest in the currently approved textbooks and Applications across the subjects/curriculum. www.bbcbitesize.com is a good educational site in the United Kingdom, possibly other countries have good sites too.

- Designate periods of times in the 5 working days of the week, to run the home school.

DEBORAH BEYIOKU

Grow your food

Growing your own food (fruits & vegetables) has both health and economic benefits. You don't need a large piece of land for it, as a small garden space will do. The time for gardening could be used as family activity time. Start with growing basic crops like...

- Tomatoes, Bell-pepper (sweet peppers), spinach and more.

- Potatoes, Beetroot, Cherries and more.

- Seeds can be purchased from retail shops like, Wilko, Asda, Lidl, and Ikea.

Keep off Name Brand Products

Keep off name brands from your shopping basket. This will save you money and help maintain healthy eating in the family. The money could be diverted to funding a family holiday and other needs.

Research has shown that named brands often has more sugar content in their food and drink.

SEVERAL MEANS OF INCOME

Stick to Necessary Spending

Sticking to spending only on necessities guided by your defined budget can help you balance your daily needs and possibly afford family treats now and then.

Tips on how to stick to necessary spending...

- Home cooking of all 3 meals daily, by that you can maintain 5 different fruit and vegetable daily and quality family time spent together cooking and eating.

- Home cooking can help provide nourishing and safe food, that will save families the waste of resourceful time spent in hospitals, the waste of time and money, especially if you live in a country without free health care.

- Home cooking will save the family money that could be put towards a bigger project, for example, starting a home business that will help generate funding for the children's higher education in future.

DEBORAH BEYIOKU

Start a Small Business

Assess yourself to identify what you enjoy doing and seek the help of experts in turning your passion into a business. A small business:

- Doesn't require large capital to start.

- Can be started from home.

- Doesn't take much quality time, away from the family.

These websites are suggested good resource for ideas:
www.mumsnet.com/family-money/saving
www.thebalance.com/budget-workshet
www.moneyhelpcenter.com
www.thegrocer.com
www.nhs.uk/live-well/eat/why
www.consumerreports.org
www.spellbrand.com
www.brandsareboring.com
www.healthyeating.org

SEVERAL MEANS OF INCOME

Wherever you are reading from, applying the guidelines in this chapter to your plan might seem a bit restrictive but it will likely be for a while until you can get your head above water. which could be in less than no time. If you live within your budget, within a short period, you could probably save enough to start your family micro-industry, and as things improve, you could employ your children and your community at large.

www.ochugroupconsultancy.com *is a good place to check for advice on starting a small business.*

DEBORAH BEYIOKU

TAKE NOTES OF PROPOSED ACTIONS PROMPTED BY THIS CHAPTER

Reader's Reflection:

_____
_____
_____
_____
_____
_____

Execution Method

_____
_____
_____
_____
_____
_____

Deadline for completion (Execute)

_____
_____
_____
_____
_____
_____

SEVERAL MEANS OF INCOME

Chapter 6

Freelance court artist

The basic requirement for becoming a court artist is the ability to draw. Therefore, it is a talent-driven career. Some have gone into education to further develop their artistic talent on different levels, while some have just continued the traditional way and never stopped. Whichever angle you choose to pursue art, the fundamental concept is that you must have been born with the talent (that is the foundation of every artist) and if you enjoy it, then you work on getting better at it through constant practice.

DEBORAH BEYIOKU

Getting better involves familiarising yourself with your environment, especially with the court which is anything but a friendly place of work. So, to gain your confidence, you need to make several trips to the court, with the purpose of gaining experience that will help improve your artistic skills over time. On deciding to make a meal out of the artist in you through the courts, acting on these ideas is the way to go.

Apply a professional Attitude

It's all about structure and the disciplinary approach in managing your work as a business. To make reasonable progress, you need to lay the grounds for accountability by:

- Purchasing your work materials ahead of your trip to the court.

- Keeping financial records to help evaluate your progress and filing your taxes.

- Arriving at court early, ideally 15 minutes before proceeding starts, to get a seat with a better view.

- Refraining from interrupting or compromising proceedings.

SEVERAL MEANS OF INCOME

Develop a unique style of work

Irrespective of your incredible talent, you need the branding to sustain a business. It's about uniqueness, the idea of providing something above board, when compared to that of your competitors, by:

- Providing quality finished work.

- Creating an impressive identity for your work.

- Provide work that depicts attention to details.

- Provide work that conveys the impression, general mood and facial expressions and gestures of the happenings during court proceedings.

Research other Court Artists

In every business, it's always advisable to associate with like-minded people as they will help to keep you 'in the know' with regards to things that really matter in the business, such as:

- Negotiating the price of your work.

- Knowing the right person or people to offer your work to for sale.

- Knowing the right way to approach the market.

DEBORAH BEYIOKU

Locate the court you want to work in

Unlike some professions, you don't need any government license, qualification or professional body membership to become a court artist, most court artists are freelanced. Therefore, you essentially must strive for work, by:

- Finding courts, to possibly locate high profile cases.

- On arrival at court, check the listing to note who the presiding Judge is likely to be.

- On arrival inform the court clerk that you are there to sketch participants during the proceeding.

- If possible, find out the court's norms depending on the Judge because while Judge 'A' may allow you in on certain terms, Judge 'B' might not.

- Traditionally, the court has a culture of no cameras or recordings allowed and some Judges are still not comfortable with even the alternative option of sketching, especially when they feel that it could compromise the case.

Source your Customers

Think about placing a value to your work and your customers agreeing to it. Traditionally, a court artist's major

SEVERAL MEANS OF INCOME

customers are the media (both publishers, broadcasters and even the internet) I suggest you extend your services to...

- Judges who would not mind a portrait of themselves while at work, something memorable for them in later years.

- Sketches of the witnesses which could be useful for lawyers on preparing for further representation, as the sketches do sometimes capture the mood of the witnesses and all involved, including jurors.

- Court artists can broaden their services by sketching and selling cartoon versions of their work.

Maintain media presence

The media now serves as a universal marketplace, reaching people across the globe. So, you could be telling your story to a wider audience through arts, by

- Creating a website with a gallery page.

- Running your own blog.

- Creating a Facebook page to interact with supporters of your work.

- Create a Twitter page to interact, network and share your work.

DEBORAH BEYIOKU

- Being on Instagram and LinkedIn to achieve the above through a different medium.

The idea is for you to go over and above what other people in your profession are doing to create jobs for yourself and possibly take on an apprentice. Even if you reside in a country where there is no such thing as a court artist, try initiating the idea. Be innovative! In this time of modern technology, we can now reach people around the world.

SEVERAL MEANS OF INCOME

TAKE NOTES OF PROPOSED ACTIONS PROMPTED BY THIS CHAPTER

Reader's Reflection:

___

Execution Method

___

Deadline for completion (Execute)

___

DEBORAH BEYIOKU

Chapter 7

Perfume making business

Are you at a soul-searching stage of your life, bored and wondering what next? Think you have been there and done that? A professional in your field but you are not passionate about what you do! Feel that something is missing, or you are just at the early stage of adulthood, not knowing where to start from? Want to do something that can give you some self-worth and an income as well; if so, then ask yourself, what puts a smile on my face?

SEVERAL MEANS OF INCOME

If the aroma of scents gets you smiling as it does for me, then here's how you can keep that smile for good, whilst making an income off it, by making these business decisions:

Research

The success of any kind of business depends largely on knowledge and information accessed before structuring, producing and marketing the product. So, it is through research that one will get a holistic idea and access to the essentials...

- Take perfume making course – that can enhance your smelling sensory and the art and science of perfume making.

    www.cotswold-perfumery.co.uk is a useful resource website.

    An understanding of the industry and organisations that are widely recognised by the UK government, in Europe and internationally. www.ctpa.org.uk, this website is another useful resource.

DEBORAH BEYIOKU

Get Perfume making Supplies

A key element is to identify and negotiate reliable sources for equipment or *Apparatus* and raw materials or *substance* with a unique idea and knowledge of commercial perfumes, dating back to the fourteenth century. For instance:

- Equipment – 1.5ml bottle/ One 200ml Erlenmeyer flask/ Gloss stirrer/ One 10ml Cylinder/ One 250ml beaker/ Three 10ml perfume bottles/One 100ml amber bottle/ Two 35ml perfume bottles.

- Raw materials – Fixative/ Dis-propylene glycol DPG/ Perfume-grad ethyl alcohol/ distilled water/ Perfume grade Cobordant.
  Check out www.chemworldfragrancefactory.com for more guidance.

Brand your product

It is important to create products and services that have a unique and identifiable presence within the chosen industry and business. To achieve this, certain things must be gotten right...

- The business name – should be suited to the products and industry, try www.thebalancesmb.com/choosing-a-great-small for ideas.

SEVERAL MEANS OF INCOME

- Designing the logo – this must be catchy and striking, as a sign on anything connected to the business, try www.freelogoservices.com/logodesignes.

Survey your market

Marketing is the moment of truth for every business, especially when venturing into a new product or industry, irrespective of your years of experience. The market these days is competitive across industries, nothing is new anymore. People tend to part with their money when a product solves their problem.

So, survey your target audience, probe their problems and communicate the solution. For guidance on conducting survey, go to www.surveymonkey.com/mp/writing-survey. Getting this early stage right, will help you identify your Unique Selling Point **(USP)**

- Advertising – Start with a message that paints a picture to your potential customers' problem, followed by the solution. Try www.ukbusinessforums.co.uk/threads for advertisement ideas.

- Social media – Create a frequent brand presence on Facebook, Instagram, Twitter and more.

DEBORAH BEYIOKU

Register your business

The Registering of a business makes it legal, identifiable and a kind of assurance to the customers. However, your structures must be right before:

- Registering a business name with as it does come with commitments and responsibilities of taxation and logistics. You can register your business at www.companieshouse.org,

- Always advisable to access Ochu Group Consultancy website for tailored holistic advice on business ideas and operations.www.ochugroupconsultancy.com

Impact on others

It is about reaching out to others, the main purpose for any business, I suppose. Extending a sense of dignity and honour by decreasing unemployment in your community through

- Taking on internships – Keeping one or more on when the programme ends.

- Organising – or keeping individuals involved with empowering projects in your community.

SEVERAL MEANS OF INCOME

This is one of the businesses that can be managed whilst still in paid employment and as it grows, you may ease-up on working for someone and gradually focus on expanding and creating more streams of income.

DEBORAH BEYIOKU

TAKE NOTES OF PROPOSED ACTIONS PROMPTED BY THIS CHAPTER

Reader's Reflection:

_____
_____
_____
_____
_____
_____

Execution Method

_____
_____
_____
_____
_____
_____

Deadline for completion (Execute)

_____
_____
_____
_____
_____
_____

SEVERAL MEANS OF INCOME

Chapter 8

Running an Indie record label

If you have the experience, good at forming partnership with other people and passion for the music industry, then you may have what it takes to own an Independent Record Label. Although it is not all that straightforward to start a business, however, with passion for the business, a sense of structure and entrepreneurship, you may be able to create a thriving empire in the music industry.

DEBORAH BEYIOKU

A good way to start is by sourcing commodity, in this case, that would be a team of music-artists. Think about the legal formalities (you may consider getting a lawyer), registering the business, sourcing funding, setting up a studio and joining music business associations.

Sourcing your Team of Music-Artist
Getting a team of music-artists on board requires a person with an influential nature, negotiating skills and the ability to make things happen (for example, getting a music-artist to sign to your label). The make-up of an Indie label team of Music-Artists should comprise of:

- Singer – the entertainer to perform the song/music.
- Songwriter – as the creative person.
- Producers - sound engineer/beats-maker.
- Band Group.
- A Disc Jockey (DJ) – to help bring the song to the notice of the public.
- Ideally a manager/Agent to mainly handle the singer's affairs.
- Label executive to oversee the running of projects.
- Event manager to help with organising live events

Finding a Lawyer

An indie record label with the zeal to succeed must have an experienced entertainment lawyer on board (with

SEVERAL MEANS OF INCOME

background / knowledge of entertainment law to help you look through the legalities) and to provide legal advice to all parties and draft contracts/agreements between parties of entertainment professionals.

Your entertainment lawyer should be expected to prepare these documents:

- Songwriter and Publisher (usually the Indie Label) Agreement "per song" – that will possibly include a fee for the songwriter and future Royalties.
- Singer and Manager Agreement.
- Singer and Publisher (Indie Label) Agreement.
- Exclusive Songwriter Team Agreement.
- Collaboration Agreement – if the need arises for a joint venture.
- Producer (beatmaker) and Indie Label Agreement.
- Lawyer and Indie Label Agreement – containing terms of payment, whether for a fee of about £150 - £350 per hour depending on experience or percentage deal or finder's fee if he found the artist or as a manager because lawyers can sometimes act as managers or as even a partner with the Indie Label.
- The lawyer will deal with copyright infringement issues for the Indie Label.
- The lawyer will deal with licensing of the songs or beats to another artist, for tv, films, advertisements, Video games and mobile phone Apps where and when required.

- A lawyer will work alongside a public relations person for certain situations.

Registering the Business

Once you have your working team in place, you should have a name in mind for your business. Check with the Companies House www.companieshouse.gov.uk to ensure that your chosen name is not already registered by someone else. On successfully registering the business, set-off to do the following needful:

- Build a website for the business, with an office phone line and email address.
- Get on social media (Twitter, Facebook, Instagram etc) make your brand known.
- Get your administrative team to handle the day to day services, like posting on your social media, taking calls, responding to mail and keeping a record of expenses.
- Have an accountant on board to help with your books, payroll and taxes.

Sourcing Funding

Funding is essential for any business, especially in the music/entertainment business where the money is needed to tidy-up deals. The best means of raising funds is to find an investor. You may entice potential investors by offering them a percentage in the profit from an event that your label will be hosting or a promotion/advertisement on your

SEVERAL MEANS OF INCOME

platforms. The label needs funding to cover basic expenses, for:

- Singers signed to the label – travel and external studio time etc.
- Arranging events.
- Paying for venues
- Equipment – computer, telephone, stationeries, microphone and more.
- Legal fees.
- Salaries.

Setting up a Studio

Gone are the days, before the 1970s to late 80s when the major music publishing companies like Sony, Universal and Varner needed expensive/extensive studios, but things have progressed from then, as an indie record label can now operate in a limited space, with comprised equipment in the form of:

- Computer with keyboard Apps – plus other needed music producing software like, the Logic Pro, Fruity Loops and Cube base.
- Internet access.
- Mobile telephone.
- The label may still engage the service of other studios – good for networking and cost-effective at times.

DEBORAH BEYIOKU

Joining Music Business Associations

In the interest of not being in isolation within the industry, keeping updated with the ongoing in the ever-evolving music industry and possibly getting help if needed, join Associations like:

- Association of Independent Music   Check out their website - www.musicindie.com/resouces/starting-a-label

- Label UK – www.izito.co.uk (they provide label templates that are used for printing labels).

- As time goes on, source and join music award organisations.

If you have a passion for the music industry, with a bit of connection and funding, this may encourage you to venture into owning an Indie Record Label, in addition to what you are presently doing. Nothing is stopping you from being an entrepreneur, rather, it will help make sure that you always have a financial door opened.

SEVERAL MEANS OF INCOME

TAKE NOTES OF PROPOSED ACTIONS PROMPTED BY THIS CHAPTER

Reader's Reflection:
_____
_____
_____
_____
_____
_____
_____

Execution Method
_____
_____
_____
_____
_____
_____

Deadline for completion (Execute)
_____
_____
_____
_____
_____
_____

DEBORAH BEYIOKU

Chapter 9

Art gallery Boss

The initial idea of owning a gallery usually comes from people with a passion for art, professional artists or people who study or work in the industry. No matter where your passion comes from, the moment you start thinking of turning that passion into a business, then it is time to turn the thought into action/reality.

SEVERAL MEANS OF INCOME

Some people go into business because they see similar business thriving and successful, but as an entrepreneur you must look beyond the thriving of the business and focus on the reason behind the progress. You need to know the basic logistic tools and actions to drive the art gallery into success, such tools are:

Business Planning

Any business with the potential to succeed should have a written business plan even if you have no intention of accessing a loan. A typical business plan starts with the name of the business/logo, explaining the running operations, marketing and growth. It should also include the kind of art that the Gallery would be dealing on. The contents should be:

Structured...

- Management – Explains ownership of shares, management profiles and staff recruitment for administration, negotiations and logistics.

- Financiers - Explains funding requirement, plan for funding, plan for growth and financial projection, analysis and budget.

DEBORAH BEYIOKU

- Income – Explains how the money will be earned by the gallery, mostly retains a commission from (50% on 2 dimensional and 40% on 3-dimensional work.

- SWOT Analysis – Explains business Strengths, Weaknesses, Opportunities and Threats.

To come up with a realistic SWOT analysis, it is ideal to survey the community where the business would be located and the industry, before completing your business plan.

Searching for Artists

The backbone of a functioning gallery is determined by the level of artist involvement; therefore, the desire of an aspiring gallery owner should be inspired by visiting art galleries and maybe museums. Attending art exhibitions, auctions and visiting art websites. It may also be useful to visit art colleges which might help you in meeting aspiring artists and, art groups in the community, including art collectors.

These are means of getting to know more artists that can display their work in the new gallery. The idea is to start with an unknown Artist, as they are more approachable, and could be accustomed to being unnoticed by major collectors. Therefore, more likely to respond quickly because they never want to pass any opportunities.

SEVERAL MEANS OF INCOME

Finding Business Premises

With all the information in your business plan and ideas gathered from your association within the art industry, whether as an art collector or an artist yourself; there would be no gallery if you don't have premises. Before deciding on a location for your gallery, consider:

- The potential benefits your gallery might gain from by being in that community.

- What the gallery can offer to the community, such as offering internships or work experience to young people.

- Accessibility of the gallery to visitors, as in the proximity from the bus stop and train station to the gallery.

- Whether the premises offer potentials for growth and expansion, should the need arise.

- Look into license restriction for the premises, very essential, should you wish to map out an area to serve food, alcohol and beverages.

- Cost of premises, if on a lease (how long), cost of business Rate to be paid to the council and commercial premises Insurance.

DEBORAH BEYIOKU

- Designing the interior/exterior of the gallery in line with your vision but be realistic with funds.

Detailed research of the premises and its surroundings will save the new gallery from any unpleasant surprises that could hinder the progression of the new gallery.

Registering the Gallery

You have chosen a name for your gallery but you have no claim to it if the business is not registered with Companies House www.companieshouse.gov.uk, either as Sole Proprietorship, Partnership or Corporation, as in limited company. You must consider these carefully so as not to make the wrong decision for you and your business. I suggest you start with:

- Checking on Company House website to ascertain the requirements for registering your business.

- Checking to confirm that your chosen business name is not already existing as a registered business.

- Familiarising yourself with the ongoing administrative requirements of Company House, such as filing the Company's yearly Confirmation Statement and Company Accounts

- Acquiring a clear understanding of HM Revenue & Customs ongoing Corporation Tax filing requirements

SEVERAL MEANS OF INCOME

or that of Self-Assessment, paying employee's tax & National Insurance contribution as well as Value Added Tax (VAT) registration threshold.

It is important to keep yourself well informed about the gallery industry. As a gallery owner you need to be involved with organisations that support arts, such as ArtGallery.co.uk (www.artgallery.co.uk) The Society of London Art dealers (www.slad.org.uk) Art Therapy in Museums and Galleries (www.atmag.org) The Association of Art & Antiques Dealers (https://Lapada.org) and a lot more, depending on where your gallery is located.

Applying Marketing Strategy

Before implementing your marketing strategy, refer to your business plan for a detailed reminder of your dream business, then ask yourself, how would this work? I have a few suggestions below:

- Keep track of the Art industry's current activities/commitments.

- Encouraging local schools' day trips to your gallery - providing the teachers and children with free vouchers.

- Encouraging family weekend outings - providing discounted vouchers through local newspapers and restaurants.

DEBORAH BEYIOKU

- Engage the public with your media presence - constant posting of events at the gallery.

- Searching for a celebrity with past or present association with the community - see if you can have him or her as a special guest to events at the gallery.

- Solicit local businesses to place an advertisement on your brochures, for a small fee.

When it comes to promoting your business, don't hesitate to play your social media joker.

Launching the Gallery

All the hard work of bringing your dream into reality is finally happening on this very important long-awaited day. To help ensure that nothing goes wrong, check that:

- Your Artist- Works are displayed, explained and priced.

- Attendance of major art collectors or buyers are confirmed

- Media Presence – Television station or Art Blogger, attendance is confirmed.

- Press Presence – Local Newspaper or Magazine attendance is confirmed.

SEVERAL MEANS OF INCOME

- Caterer – Arrange to provide light refreshments.
- MC (Master of ceremony), Projector for slides and Background music are all in place.
- Local businesses and the College Art department – attendance is confirmed.

Oh! The 'icing on the cake' could be the presence of the Mayor, the local councillor, a local Member of Parliament, or the local Celebrity?

DEBORAH BEYIOKU

TAKE NOTES OF PROPOSED ACTIONS PROMPTED BY THIS CHAPTER

Reader's Reflection

_____
_____
_____
_____
_____

Execution Method

_____
_____
_____
_____
_____

Deadline for completion (Execute)

_____
_____
_____
_____
_____

SEVERAL MEANS OF INCOME

Chapter 10

Business to Business Teamwork

Working together for "profitability" is an expected common goal of every business. When in search of such a goal, businesses reach out to complement each other, to increase their profit margin in the long run. By signposting and referring their customers to purchase other businesses' products or services that their business does not provide, and in turn they expect them to do the same. This can be achieved by forming special arrangements between businesses.

DEBORAH BEYIOKU

Businesses need to pay less attention to unhealthy competition and take the necessary actions to work together as a team. Some of the ways that businesses could work together are:

Associations
Two or more companies (in similar industries) coming together to endorse each other's business with the aim of achieving a common goal. It is advisable to start with drafting an Associate's Agreement/Contract that states the benefits, possible risks, responsibilities of each member and the consequences of a likely breach of the contract.

Joint Ventures
Ordinarily known as JV, a formed temporary partnership of 2 or more businesses with a common beneficial interest to share in the profit, cost and even risks, should that occur. It is always prudent to specify the type of Joint venture you plan to get involved with, as there may be legal implications. The 3 common joint ventures are Limited Co-operation, Separate Joint Business and Business Partnership.

Planned Alliances
Planned Alliances is the coming together of businesses to form a group with a strategic aim of benefiting each other's business. As the group expands, they may decide to have different meeting zones for proximity. Such meetings are normally held monthly, and members are offered the opportunity to introduce/present their business to the group, hoping for a referral from members or even direct business deals between members. To join such an alliance in the United Kingdom, search www.business-buzz.org for the

SEVERAL MEANS OF INCOME

nearest one to you. There might be equivalent alliances in other countries, or you can search www.ochugroupconsultancy.com to inquire on how to set-up your local Planned Alliance.

Affiliates Marketing
This seems to be common with large organisations engaging individuals and smaller businesses to create awareness for their products and services. Possibly offering financial rewards when purchases are made through the affiliate links. Affiliate marketing is a striving and profiting home-based business, common with www.amazon.com, www.ebay.com and others.

Conjunctions
This is the unifying of businesses, possibly with a common interest in promoting their business. Each party presents innovative ideas in a manner that will prompt the other party to diversify their business to help maximise both party's profit. An example of companies in conjunctions is www.secretescape.com, www.cheapflights.com and www.opodo.com, all booking flight tickets, hotels and car rentals.

Deal Making
This is mostly introduced to businesses through consultants, informing both parties of how they can increase their customers whilst saving on advertisement cost, by striking deals with another business. An example could be where a bicycle store employs the service of a health and wellbeing consultant to help point out the dangers of unhealthy

DEBORAH BEYIOKU

lifestyle and environmental pollution, with the aim of getting that business to accept discount vouchers for the staff and customers to purchase bicycles/accessories from the store. Deal-making is mostly common amongst local businesses.

Although the advice on business to business teamwork might seem a bit difficult due to not being sure of which of the applications is best suited for your business, experience has shown that they produce almost the same result for the businesses involved. It is worth trying out by businesses wanting to maximise their profit margins. If you are faced with the problem of applying the preferred method, contact Ochu Group on www.ochugroupconsultancy.com for guidance on a strategy to suit your business growth.

SEVERAL MEANS OF INCOME

TAKE NOTES OF PROPOSED ACTIONS PROMPTED BY THIS CHAPTER

Reader's Reflection
_____
_____
_____
_____
_____
_____
_____

Execution Method
_____
_____
_____
_____
_____
_____

Deadline for completion (Execute)
_____
_____
_____
_____
_____
_____

DEBORAH BEYIOKU

Chapter 11

Keeping your business financially afoot

Even the most thought out business strategy could go wrong if all efforts in generating cash for the business fails. It could be due to a saturated market, austerity because of change in government/policy or a yet to be identified bad marketing strategy. Whatever may be the cause, an emerging low battery in cash flow requires a jump-start.

SEVERAL MEANS OF INCOME

A good way of injecting cash into the business could be by taking an inventory of your old stock and making the decision to free your store of old stock. Here are some of the fastest means of keeping a business financially afoot...

Freeing your store off old stock

It's a way of using 'one stone to kill two birds' as old stock can be used to boost the sale of unsellable stocks, by using it as:

- Incentives for customers - when other purchases are made.

- Charitable giving – a gesture of goodwill is always good for business by providing some of your product and services to support their noble course.

- Sponsorship – a way of reaching out to other businesses asking them to sponsor your ongoing project.

- Bulks sell – to people selling from the back of the van at street markets or even the pound stores.

Offering a discount to your debtors

Checking your books to identify lingering debts and offering to meet the debtors halfway, by:

- Writing your debtors to pay back a certain percentage and the rest will be forfeited.
- Writing your debtors to make an affordable payment arrangement with them.

Offering Gift Vouchers to Customers

It is a workable way of injecting cash into business as this will encourage customers to:

- make purchases that they normally would not have afforded or ordinarily purchased.
- Use the voucher in place of normal gift or cash and it is prepaid to your business.

Offering Subscriptions

Subscriptions are another method that businesses can use to set-up permanent means of income, as in the form of:

- Monthly subscription for newsletters.
- Free delivery for subscribers.
- Next day delivery for subscribers.
- Customers get a discount for making a full year payment.

SEVERAL MEANS OF INCOME

Offering Special Deals to Customers

In the business world, a special deal is the 'magic word' used for boosting sales as it draws in:

- New customers – bringing in more money.
- Retains existing customers and referrals.
- Customers' attention tends to be drawn to other products while checking the special deal.
- Tend to allow customers extra money to even spend on other items from your business.

Venturing into new markets

The starting point is to check who your advertisements are reaching and if your present methods of advert is not increasing the customer number and capital generation, then it's about time to redirect your method of reaching your target audience by:

- Reviewing the services of your **(PR)** Public Relations person
- Making maximum use of social media
- Stepping beyond your demographics

To avoid frequent low cash flow, note and systemize the workable cash-generating ideas and keep initiating more responsible moral and legal avenues of generating funds with the aim of injecting the required cash into your business.

DEBORAH BEYIOKU

TAKE NOTES OF PROPOSED ACTIONS PROMPTED BY THIS CHAPTER

Reader's Reflection

_____
_____
_____
_____
_____
_____

Execution Method

_____
_____
_____
_____
_____
_____

Deadline for completion (Execute)

_____
_____
_____
_____
_____
_____

SEVERAL MEANS OF INCOME

Chapter 12

Sustaining your business

Due to financial constraint, most businesses tend to start from the homes and as the business progresses, we begin to weigh our options as to the pros and cons of running a business from home. The issue of separating office hours from time with the family, issue of privacy, possibility of customers and staff coming to your home, the issue of separating personal possessions from that of the business and even finances (the complication of insurance, Utility Bills, Council Tax and Business Rate), especially when filing taxes.

Deciding to get premises solely for business should be the first step to making your business official to the public. Therefore, one must apply, structure, consistency, tenacity and accountability in acquiring the necessities for sustaining your business...

Business Premises

Points to consider when looking for a business premises:

- Your business plans, checking your business plan to ensure that the premises accommodate your plans for growth.

- Your kind of business choose an area that accommodates the demographics of your customers or clientele.

- Your finances to help you on whether to decide on purchase of a leasehold or freehold property. Purchasing a premise requires immense capital and commitment; and I wouldn't recommend for a start-up business except you have the capital. There is also the option of a property license, ideal for new businesses as it is much easier to terminate the agreement, should your circumstance change. The downside could also be the Landlord issuing you notice when you are not prepared to move.

SEVERAL MEANS OF INCOME

Whichever one you settle for, make sure your activities in the premises does comply with building regulations.

I would recommend renting or leasing, again, considering your capital. Whichever of these paths you choose, consider taking up the services of a solicitors to advice on the terms of the premises.

Equipment Management

As you move the business to the next level, possibly from the home to a solely business space, the idea is to acquire the very needed items that will help your business function efficiently.

Tips...

- Consider which items you are better off getting on lease or rent, rather than purchase. Depending on the business, vehicles, printers, industrial machines could be rented whilst such basics like chairs, desk, shelves, stationery could be purchased.

- Equipment must be maintained, and staff adequately trained to use it.

- Regarding the use of machines and computers, stick to the related regulations and confirm with www.hse.gov.uk if in doubt.

- Decide whether to subcontract, instead of purchasing and training staff to use certain equipment, if it will help lower running cost.

Owning equipment is advantageous because it's an asset but remember, the value depreciates over time, so it makes business sense to only purchase necessary equipment that makes financial sense.

Health and Safety (H&S)

The Health and Safety law exists to protect employees and employers alike. Both employers and employees are responsible for making sure that the possibility of an accident in the workplace is reduced to the minimum.

Policies…

- Openly display your Health & Safety Regulations as relevant to your type of business. Remember to appoint a Health and Safety officer for the company.

- Provide an accessible first aid box, appoint a trained first aider to perform first aid including Cardiopulmonary Resuscitation (CPR), do frequent checks and restock the box as required.

SEVERAL MEANS OF INCOME

- Accident record book must be provided, with dates, time, the name of the injured (including customers and visitors) and a detailed account of the incident that occurred, even very minor ones.
- Report certain incidents like, death/serious injury, work-related illness and incident that caused staff to be off work for over 3weeks, to the Health and Safety Executive or to your local council.

The level of care will depend on your type of business, obviously, an industry with heavy machinery will require more policies in place.

Fire Protection & Waste Management

Having acquired a premise for the business, a fire risk assessment is needed, to demonstrate that proper fire safety control is in place. Your local fire safety officer based at your local fire stations can guide the process.

Requirements...

- To meet the standard, adequate escape route and meeting point must be provided.

- Fire alarms and enough firefighting equipment, including emergency lightening and safe storage for flammable materials.

All waste must be properly separated and disposed of. When being removed from premises, waste disposal transfer notes must be completed and kept for 2years; 3years if it is toxic and hazardous waste.

Stock and Supplies

Supplies and Stock is crucial to any business, therefore, sourcing the right supplier and negotiating for consistent, quality and high standard raw material is necessary. It is prudent to get several quotes from suppliers, then evaluate all and decide which to negotiate and settle for.

By...

- Prioritizing your needs for the material and constantly reviewing your suppliers and their services.
- Check to ensure that your suppliers are reliable, consistent and punctual.
- Only start negotiating when you are certain that it is what you want and confirm agreed terms in writing.

To be on the safe side with your business, retain two suppliers at least. Be well informed and updated about changes in government legislation and policies relating to your type of business, including that of your source of raw material for your stocks, should it be imported.

SEVERAL MEANS OF INCOME

Staff Structure

The intended structure of staff within your business should be outlined in your business plan, from Director or partnership (assuming it's a limited company) associates and secretary, stating their names, qualification, and related experiences/knowledge.

Routinely, check to update your business plan, concerning:

- Key Personnel leaving and joining the business.
- acquired new skills and qualifications after a completed training program or course.
- The changing market, new technology and business expansion requiring further staff recruitment.

Sometimes, it is cost-effective to sub-contract missing and needed skills in the company, however, quantify the odds as to whether it's' better spent on staff training to avert skill shortages within the company.

DEBORAH BEYIOKU

TAKE NOTES OF PROPOSED ACTIONS PROMPTED BY THIS CHAPTER

Reader's Reflection

_____
_____
_____
_____
_____

Execution Method

_____
_____
_____
_____
_____

Deadline for completion (Execute)

_____
_____
_____
_____
_____

SEVERAL MEANS OF INCOME

Chapter 13

Your business gold

We are familiar with the old quote "New friends are silver old friends are gold." Applying that to your business, your existing customers are gold and are to be retained by any means legally and morally necessary. A retained customer is equally a source of informal referral because a satisfied customer will most likely tell family and friends, and people are more comfortable doing business based on the recommendation of others that have experienced the service or products.

It is easier to gain more customers when you have a good method of retaining the ones you already have. These strategic methods are certain to keep customers coming back and bringing new ones too...

Conducting Frequent Surveys

For both formal and informal survey, these websites might help (http://www.questionpro.com, or https://www.surveymonkey.co.uk) as a form of equipping your staff into providing quality service, conducting surveys over the phone and providing customers with service information. Your survey might explore these areas:

- Maximum of 5 minutes on-hold time, over the phone.

- Rate the service you received on a scale of 1 to 5.

- How likely are you to recommend our products and/or services to family and friends?

Make attempts to find out how your product/service meets your customer's needs.

Do not be desperate

Being desperate is perceived as aggressive salesmanship, talking over customers and not taking time to listen to them, rushing them to make an order or close a deal,(https://www.gooddealshark.com) politely allow the customer time to;

SEVERAL MEANS OF INCOME

- Think through what they want and if not forthcoming, gently send a reminder.

- Respond as to whether their inquiries have been satisfactorily dealt with.

- Examine their understanding of your product and services, by reading out the sales policy to them if necessary.

Strategize Negotiating Process

Whether you are buying from your Suppliers or selling to your customers, it is important to have well-trained people for the job and a precise but unique process of negotiating, for more on negotiation visit [http://www.moneycrashers.com/negotiation] suited to your business. To negotiate effectively you need to:

- Have a maximum that you are willing to pay to suppliers and the minimum you are willing to sell.

- Be willing to explain why you are sticking to a price.

- Make allowances for offers and be precise in stating the period of the offer and what you expect back for the offer, for example, reduced price for bulk purchase.

The key to a satisfying negotiation is getting the other party in a good mood. Nothing spoils a meeting like turning up late. So, start by being punctual and well prepared to provide reasons for your decisions.

Enhance Services/products at intervals

Create a habit of finding out what your closest competitors are offering and devise a means of doing better whilst being cost-effective. A good way to do this is by visiting www.startupbizhub.com/how-competition-affects-business.)

Relate this to your customers by;

1. Getting to know your customers as much as possible and device when best to introduce a new idea of service/product.
2. Showing your customers how the improvements would be beneficial to them.

It is important to set-up a procedure of revisiting any new idea/innovation to the business, to see how profitable it is to you. Every customer wants an answer to that unasked question of what do I gain?

Prioritise all Sections of the Business

Front desk reception, working as the face of the business at the first approach to a place of business.

Telephone marketing, every phone call to or from customers should be handled politely by all levels of staff, good telephone manners will help to create more business

SEVERAL MEANS OF INCOME

opportunities. It doesn't matter whether it is an existing or new customer.

It costs nothing to be polite, so staffs should be polite to customers, irrespective of the quantity that the customer intends to purchase.

Consistent and cordial customer care will deter your customers from looking elsewhere.

For more ideas on every section of what increases profit, try, https://www.entrepreneur.com /article/ Placing importance 235768.

Know your Products/Services

All staff needs to have a clear knowledge of the products and services your business offers.

Try www.business.qld.gov.au/running-business/marketing-al for updating your staff about any changes within your business. As well as information about changes in products or services. They need to know:

- Promotions, when it starts and ends, and availability.

- What the customer must do, to benefit from the ongoing offer.

- Pre-equip the staff on possible questions from the customer and when unsure, ask management, to avoid inconsistency or misinformation, getting things right will help maintain customers' trust and business integrity.

They may deliver the service with confidence, as in displaying a convincing and concerned attitude. A little reward to your staff goes a long way to encouraging them to feel included in the business instead of just feeling like an ordinary employee with no interest in the business.

Staff/team may feel motivated if there is a reciprocal benefit to staff from increased profit/sales for the business.

SEVERAL MEANS OF INCOME

TAKE NOTES OF PROPOSED ACTIONS PROMPTED BY THIS CHAPTER

Reader's Reflection
_____
_____
_____
_____
_____
_____

Execution Method
_____
_____
_____
_____
_____
_____

Deadline for completion (Execute)
_____
_____
_____
_____
_____
_____

Chapter 14

You can be rich and happy

"Money does not buy happiness" contrary to that phrase, I would say.... You can be rich and happy, depending on how you choose to make the money or what you deem as happiness. The absence of either one can only result in sadness, stress, depression, uncertainty, hopelessness, the breakdown of family units or relationships, which may lead to serious illnesses.

SEVERAL MEANS OF INCOME

I would recommend the following in order to have a balanced happy lifestyle by achieving both good qualities if we apply these ideas:

Avoid negative ideas

If you want to make headway in life, it may help to adopt a "He who dares wins" attitude and ability to spot the typical signs of negative ideas, like...

- It is not possible – meaning, the world has exhausted all smart ideas and there can't be any new ones.

- Be realistic – meaning, don't be innovative.

- You can't do it – meaning, you are not smart enough.

- Be content and happy with your life – meaning, don't be ambitious, just stay at the same position for the rest of your life, don't move.

Avoid sharing your business ideas with people that make such comments above, even if they are family, because they may be lazy and redundant brains with demotivating persona.

Consider how your business can benefit others

Treating others with respect and dignity, without prejudice, it is a mind-set that will make you put people in the equation when planning your business, this you can do by...

- Implementing a training programme for unskilled people.

- Awarding them with a certificate at the end of the training.

- Donating your time to a good course, i.e. a charity of your choice.

- Accessing new business growth methods and impacting on your community.

Most people who have been successful in business acknowledge the benefits of respecting people that work in their business.

Identify the market gap in your community

This involves doing your research to identify the under-provided services or product in your community and devising a means of filling the gap, by:

- Conducting a marketing survey within your business community before starting the business.

- Joining business clubs to know what is currently trending in the business world.

- Joining business discussions on social media.

- Attending trade fairs, seminars, workshops and events.

SEVERAL MEANS OF INCOME

Business is not a game for those who fear failure and while going down the route of this precocious method does not guarantee success of a business, but it can increase the possibilities of success and gaining both positive and not so positive experiences. Whichever way you choose to perceive experience, the key thing is that they are very important lessons of life. A wise person will learn from it and move on to do better.

Identify employment gap in your community

It is usually a plus to have your business within a community where money circulates amongst the larger percentage of the population and this is only possible where businesses aim to reduce unemployment level to a minimum across board. To support such an idea, you need to:

- Know and identify the demographic of the unemployed in your community.

- Compare the amount of registered active job seekers to available jobs.

- Take account of the crime level in the local area and the demographic of the perpetrators and victims alike.

- Often, a high level of unemployment among youths could result in high crime rates.

Taking these into consideration may alert you to the employment gap that needs to be filled.

Love your business

Here is the actual route to happiness, no one that loves what they do for a living will be unhappy. So, the process of loving your business is by...

- Creating a harmonious working environment that promotes happiness for staff.
- Providing good customer service to improve customer satisfaction and increase revenue.
- Designating and respecting your time for leisure because it reduces stress.
- Being on top of your game in your line of business.

It is all about prioritising, structuring, methodising and balancing each one of the things that you are involved in.

Make time for family and friends

This is the most important part of the reason for life, we make money to enjoy it with our family and friends. The source of our happiness is knowing that our loved ones are happy. So, you should consider placing your business and family at an equal level of importance, by...

- Making time for family meals - an opportunity to share your daily experiences.
- Making time for family holidays.

SEVERAL MEANS OF INCOME

- Making time to attend children's school events.
- Attending social events with family and friends.

Finally, have a stringent attitude towards your business accounts and the budgets for running your home/private life. Develop a pattern of planning activities ahead and you will never be caught wanting. When in doubt or faced with a task beyond your area of expertise, seek professional help, bearing in mind that whoever solves the problem that you cannot solve by yourself, absolutely deserves to be paid for the services rendered. Applying and balancing these may place you in the categories of 'rich and happy' people. Don't we all want that?

For holistic progression of your business or start-up, find the solution in www.ochugroupconsultancy.com

DEBORAH BEYIOKU

TAKE NOTES OF PROPOSED ACTIONS PROMPTED BY THIS CHAPTER

Reader's Reflection

_____
_____
_____
_____
_____
_____

Execution Method

_____
_____
_____
_____
_____

Deadline for completion (Execute)

_____
_____
_____
_____
_____
_____

SEVERAL MEANS OF INCOME

My Final Thoughts

This book has looked at the creation of income from the grassroots. If you were indecisive on a career path, starting your own business or creating extra sources of generating more money. Most of this procrastinating nature is drawn from fear of the unknown or fear of failure may because you have made unsuccessful business decisions in the past, but remember this:

"Never think of your past, it brings tear: Never think of your future, it brings fear; just think of your present, And cherish your life" inspirational quote

Now begin to execute your ideas from your passions or experiences, if you are already running a business, now you can identify the some of the problem and apply the solution, don't waste time apportioning blame.

If you are presently in paid employment you may realise that you need financial independence to give you more time with your loved ones, which is the actual accomplishment of peace and joy that we all hope for.

You may be retired and feel that it is too late to make-up on the inadequate time spent with your now grown children and next to nothing available funds you had to spend on them as children. Use your passion and experiences to accomplish financial and time independence. Whilst at it, happily remedy the time you lost with your now adult children by

DEBORAH BEYIOKU

spending quality time with your grandchildren. If you couldn't be a fantastic parent! Work hard on being a fantastic grandparent!

Your motivation might even be drawn from the happenings around you, it is never too late, so long as you are alive and healthy. Let nothing hold you back, especially age, just think of **Captain Tom Moore** (now 'Sir' amongst other titles and accolades), a man driven by his love for humanity at the outbreak of Covid-19. Ignoring his age (99years), he set to raise £1000.00 for the (NHS) National Health Service, before his 100years birthday by completing 100 laps but ended up in raising over £33m for the NHS. More people are now motivated by his actions.

The American Motivational Speaker, Author and coach **Tony Robbins** once said:

"No matter how many mistakes you make, or how slow you progress, you are still way ahead of everyone who isn't trying."

I'm hopeful that you will act on the idea of starting some uncommon lines of business or talents mentioned in this book. This book has also provided suggestions to sustain existing businesses and where to get direct expert assistance to help your business achieve it's expected aim.

As you have noticed, there are no boring moments in this book, no confusing technicalities or language. By now you are impacted with the clarity and easily applicable methods

SEVERAL MEANS OF INCOME

that this book directs you the reader to implement. You will be impacting on your communities by making your contribution to reduce unemployment and increasing good health and wellbeing by starting a business that could progress enough to provide employment. Echoing my favourite quotes from Martin Luther king Jr. –

'Life's most persistent and urgent question is, 'What are you doing for others?"

Money is good but I equally focus on advocating for joy through the work I do for my client as a consultant in the quest to provide solutions "Troubleshooting" to problems. As you have noticed this book takes you beyond just making money but also emphasizes on the importance of the inner joy and this is achievable by raising people as in the form of impacting on them. That is the greatest accomplishment in life, more than money. It creates a safe and healthy community.

Check out Ochu website for more insight on how to further achieve financial freedom and free up your time and also how to make an impact in your community. Go to www.ochugroupconsultancy.com to set the ball rolling

I presume that you have been making notes on the reflection pages, after each chapter.

Now you need to put into perspective, the crucial issue 'finances' and this book has provided you with a starting point....

DEBORAH BEYIOKU

1) **What is your present total income?** List all the sources, if more than one. Not just income from wages, including financial worth of gifts and time.

SEVERAL MEANS OF INCOME

2) **What is your present total monthly expenditure?** *List all your outgoings, as much as you can remember. Including miscellaneous expenses.*

DEBORAH BEYIOKU

3) ***How do you spend your time?*** List how you spend your time (Monday - Friday) remember the saying "time is money." Including 'me time' if you haven't yet figured that out.

SEVERAL MEANS OF INCOME

*4) **What is your proposed innovation and location?** List your business and where you wish to place **it**. If you can think of it! You can do it!*

5) **What is your expected result?** List what you expect to achieve with your business. For example, the best coach, speaker, publisher in your community!

SEVERAL MEANS OF INCOME

6) ***What is your value?*** *List what you think that you are worth for the services you plan to provide in your line of businesses, as an entrepreneur in the making. Including what you would like to be known for in your community and possibly the globe.*

DEBORAH BEYIOKU

> " Treat problems like a guest, only you can decide how long they stay for "

"This has been an eye opener to how I intend to approach my business. Deborah has reminded me that the power that drives success is within me"

Yezzi Yezzir
Musician & Security Business owner
★★★★★

"We were going through a tough period trying to figure how to expand our business, this book has now been the reason as to why we have a successful cafe adjacent to our bakery, we couldn't have done it without the gems found in several means of income!

Ian Daimant
Bakery Shop owner
★★★★★

Printed in Great Britain
by Amazon